Psychology

CONTENTS

Written by Belynder Walia

Collins

1 INTRODUCTION

Welcome to the extraordinary world of psychology! Psychology gives us a key to a fascinating place where you can uncover the secrets of the human mind, discovering the thoughts, feelings and behaviours that make each of us unique. Psychology helps us understand why we laugh, cry or get excited. It's the ultimate adventure in self-discovery, allowing us to understand ourselves and others in new and intriguing ways.

Have you ever wondered what makes you happy when playing with your best friends? Or why your heart races when you're scared of something, like spiders or the dark? Psychology gives us explanations for these mysteries. Think of your brain as a giant jigsaw puzzle with thousands of pieces, and psychology is the tool that helps you fit all the pieces together. It's like being an investigator, solving the mysteries of the mind!

So, what exactly is psychology, and why is it so interesting? Imagine your brain is a superhero headquarters. Just like superheroes have extraordinary powers, your brain has incredible abilities too. Psychology helps you discover these superpowers, understanding why you get butterflies in your stomach before a big test or why you feel over the moon when you win a game. It's about figuring out how our brains work, why we experience different feelings, and how to use this knowledge to live happier and better lives.

Are you ready?

Then let's dive into an exploration of the mind.

How we explore the mysteries of the mind

As we embark on our adventure into the world of psychology, we'll meet incredible people who have changed how we understand human behaviour. From Wilhelm Wundt, the brainy trailblazer who founded psychology experiments, to Ivan Pavlov, the canine trainer extraordinaire who discovered how dogs respond to familiar sounds, we'll learn more about them later. Their ideas are fascinating, and they've each provided a unique **insight** into our understanding of human behaviour.

Next, we'll nose-dive deep into the brainy stuff. We're about to peek inside our heads to understand how our thoughts and feelings shape who we are. Put on your detective hat, and solve the mystery of why we experience sensations such as anger, happiness, sadness, or even loneliness! Once you've got to grips with your thoughts and feelings, it's time to understand how those feelings influence our reactions: why do we feel confident in some situations and nervous in others? Get ready for mind-bending tricks, like optical illusions that'll make you go, "Whoa, how does that even work?"

Finally, we'll explore all the fantastic jobs in psychology. From helping kids with schoolwork to supporting people with their feelings, psychology can truly improve the world.

2 INFLUENTIAL FIGURES

Meet the mind masters

In 1879, Wilhelm Wundt set up the first psychology **laboratory** in Germany. A super-curious man, like the Sherlock Holmes of the brain, he asked some wondrous questions. Maybe you wonder the same things:

WHY DO WE SLEEP?

WHAT MAKES US AFRAID?

Around the same time, other brilliant minds were working on their own groundbreaking research. Ivan Pavlov discovered why dogs drool when they hear a bell, showing how our brains connect sounds to actions. Sigmund Freud, the dream detective, explored the wild world of dreams. Jean Piaget, the magician of childhood, discovered that kids think in totally different ways to adults.

Then there was Anna Freud, who studied how children manage their feelings, and Mary Whiton Calkins, a trailblazer for women in science. BF Skinner discovered how rewards and consequences shape our actions – think of how you feel when you get a gold star for doing your homework! Melanie Klein used playtime to help kids express their **emotions**, while Carl Rogers, the kindness champion, showed that **empathy** and listening can help people develop. Mamie Phipps Clark used dolls to study how kids understand race, shining a light on how people can influence ideas.

These marvellous brain detectives revolutionised our understanding of the mind, proving that curiosity and determination can uncover incredible secrets.

Why were the pioneers famous?

These psychologists each had a unique way of exploring the mind. They weren't always the best of friends, but they knew about each other's work and sometimes had friendly debates. Just like you might wonder why your friends or teachers behave a certain way, these brain detectives tried to understand why people think and act the way they do.

The brainy trailblazer:
Wilhelm Wundt (1832–1920)

Wilhelm Wundt was famous for setting up the world's first psychology laboratory in 1879 in Leipzig, Germany. He conducted experiments to explore people's thoughts and senses. One famous test involved volunteers pressing a button when they heard a sound, showing how quickly our brains react to things.

Wilhelm Wundt

Wundt's studies showed that our thoughts and senses could be measured scientifically, which was a huge step forward for psychology.

FUN FACT

Wundt wrote over 50,000 pages in his lifetime, which is the equivalent of filling several bookshelves, with his ideas about how our brains work. Imagine bookcases packed with just his discoveries – that's how much Wundt wrote!

The dog trainer extraordinaire: Ivan Pavlov (1849–1936)

Ivan Pavlov became famous for a fascinating experiment with dogs that changed how we think about learning.

Pavlov was the first person to study this behavioural learning method. It's called "classical **conditioning**", which is when we teach our brains to do something without even realising it's happening. Here's what happened: Pavlov noticed that when he rang a bell every time he fed his dogs, eventually just hearing the bell made them drool, even if there was no food around. This showed that animals (and people, too!) could learn to connect different things in their minds.

Ivan Pavlov

Pavlov's discovery showed us how our brains can be trained to link different things, like sounds and actions. This helped scientists understand how we learn new things and why we react in specific ways.

Similar to how you might feel happy when you hear the ice-cream van music, Pavlov's dogs learnt to feel excited when they heard the bell.

FUN FACT

Pavlov noticed that his dog would start drooling whenever he entered the room, even before any experiments began. Pavlov's dog was so excited to see him that it couldn't help but slobber everywhere. Yuck! Pavlov realised this funny reaction could be studied, leading to his famous experiments on conditioning.

The dream detective:
Sigmund Freud (1856–1939)

Sigmund Freud was famous for exploring dreams to uncover hidden thoughts and feelings. He believed dreams were secret messages from our minds, revealing our deepest fears, wishes and worries. Freud's special way

Sigmund Freud

of helping people, called **psychoanalysis**, involved having a deep conversation with a professional to understand yourself better. His work showed that our **unconscious** mind influences our thoughts and behaviours, and that by talking about our dreams and feelings, we can understand and solve our problems. This approach changed forever how therapists and doctors help people with their mental health.

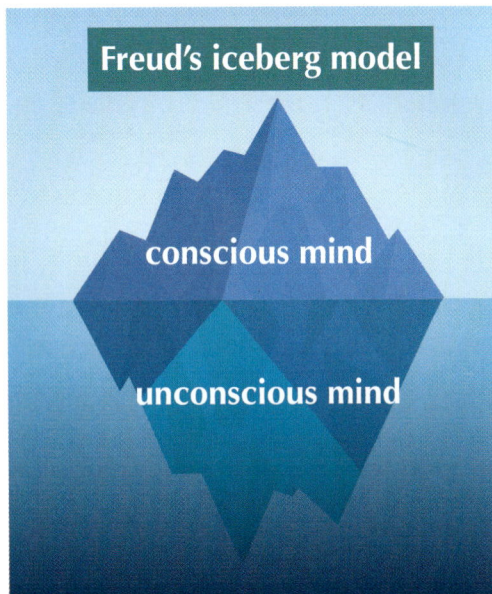

Freud's iceberg model

conscious mind

unconscious mind

Freud's discoveries shone a flashlight into the hidden corners of our minds, teaching us that understanding our dreams can help us understand ourselves better.

Freud solved the mysteries of the mind, helping people feel happier and healthier. His work was a giant leap forward in understanding how our minds work and how we can care for our brains.

FUN FACT

Freud wasn't just into studying the mind – he loved **archaeology**, too! He collected over 2,000 ancient artefacts, including old statues and coins.

The child psychologist:
Anna Freud (1895–1982)

Anna Freud was famous not because she was the daughter of Sigmund Freud, but because she focused on how children manage their feelings. She founded child psychoanalysis and developed ways to understand and support

Anna Freud

children through play and observation. Her work showed that psychologists could learn much about how kids think and feel by watching and playing with them. This helped create better ways to support children with their emotions and mental health.

Anna believed psychologists could gain valuable insights into children's minds by observing them in their natural play environment. She set up a nursery school in London where she could watch children play and learn about their feelings and behaviours. This playful approach was groundbreaking and showed that understanding children's responses is essential for helping them become happy and healthy adults. Her discoveries have helped countless kids understand and manage their thoughts, proving that playtime can be powerful.

FUN FACT

Anna learnt most of what she knew, not in school, but from interesting guests who visited her home. She picked up several languages from them, including Hebrew, German, English, French, and Italian!

The mind magician of childhood:
Jean Piaget (1896–1980)

Jean Piaget was famous for studying how kids' brains grow and change. He found that children's brains work differently from adults. In one experiment, he showed children two glasses of juice, one tall and one short, both containing the same amount of juice. Kids thought the tall glass had more juice in it, showing that young brains focus more on appearances than reality.

Jean Piaget

Piaget discovered that children go through stages of thinking as they grow. He realised that children are effectively little scientists, always exploring and learning about the world around them. His work helped teachers and parents understand that kids need varied support and learning experiences at different ages. Piaget's work and ideas continue to shape how we teach and understand children, making him the ultimate mind magician of childhood.

FUN FACT

Piaget published his first scientific report when he was just ten years old! Imagine writing about science while other kids are playing with toys. Piaget was a child genius, solving mysteries about snails. While his friends were busy collecting marbles, he was collecting important facts.

The self-psychology pioneer:
Mary Whiton Calkins (1863–1930)

Mary Whiton Calkins bravely stood up for women who were not encouraged to be scientists. Despite being denied a PhD from Harvard University because she was a woman, she never gave up. She protested this **exclusion** by continuing her research and teaching with determination.

Mary Whiton Calkins

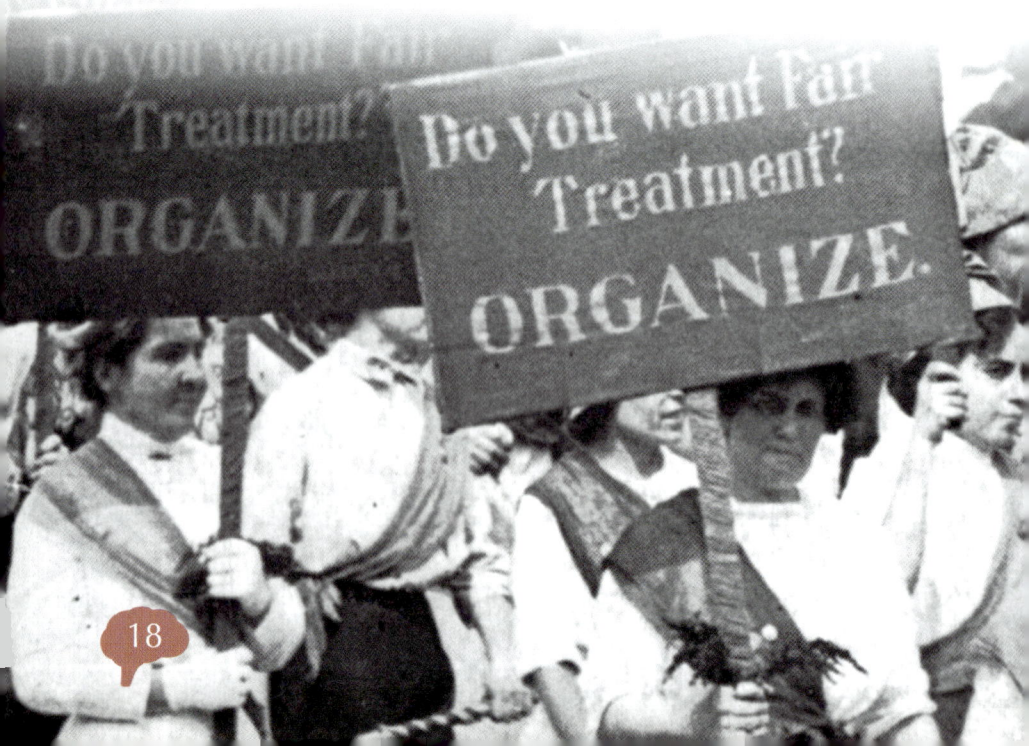

Do you want Fair Treatment? ORGANIZE.

Calkins focused on studying the **conscious self** and how what we think about ourselves influences our behaviour. Her hard work paid off when she became the first female president of the American Psychological Association (APA), a famous organisation for psychologists.

Calkins' commitment and courage helped change the world of psychology. She showed that our thoughts about ourselves shape our actions and that understanding this can help us improve our lives. Her achievements remind us that no matter the challenges, we can achieve great things with determination and hard work. Calkins truly was a **pioneer**, inspiring many to follow in her footsteps and pursue their dreams.

FUN FACT

Despite many obstacles, Calkins became the first woman to lead a group of brilliant minds. Calkins broke barriers and paved the way for future generations of female scientists, showing everyone that women can be outstanding scientists, too!

The play therapy innovator: Melanie Klein (1882–1960)

Melanie Klein was famous for a super idea: using playtime to help kids share their feelings. She showed that toys, like dolls and cars, aren't just for fun – they're also great for understanding emotions. Both Melanie Klein and Anna Freud were pioneers in child psychology, but they had unique approaches. While Anna Freud focused on how children manage their emotions and used play for observation, Klein took it further by using play as a direct method to help kids express their deepest feelings. This made Klein a big deal in child psychoanalysis and play therapy, assisting psychologists to understand kids' thoughts and emotions better.

Imagine solving your problems by playing with your favourite toys. Thanks to their groundbreaking work, therapy can be as fun and exciting as an adventure into your own imagination!

Melanie Klein

For example, if a child plays with dolls by making them argue or fight, Klein might see this as a sign that the child is experiencing anger or conflict. If a child carefully nurtures a toy animal, it might show their need for love and care. By observing these play scenarios, Klein could understand the child's emotions and help them discuss and manage these concerns during therapy sessions.

FUN FACT

Klein, born in Vienna, Austria, went on a big adventure in 1926 when she moved to England. Despite all her challenges as a woman in the early 1900s, she became a superstar in psychology, especially for her radical work with children. Her ideas have been helping people understand how kids think and feel ever since.

The behaviour scientist: BF Skinner (1904–1990)

BF Skinner was famous for studying operant conditioning, which is basically learning through rewards and consequences. He used a special box, now called the Skinner Box, to show how this works. In his experiments,

BF Skinner

he put animals like pigeons and rats inside the box, and the animals would get a treat when they pressed a lever or pecked a key. Over time, the animals learnt that they could press the lever or peck the key to get more scrumptious food.

Skinner's work helped us understand how rewards can encourage good behaviour and how consequences can stop bad behaviour. Thanks to his studies, we know more about how to train pets, teach students, and even build good habits ourselves. Skinner's ideas help us improve and develop.

FUN FACT

Skinner once trained pigeons to play ping-pong! Yes, you read that right – ping-pong! He showed that even birds could learn to do something fun and unexpected with the right rewards. Imagine a pigeon scoring points in a ping-pong game!

The kindness champion:
Carl Rogers (1902–1987)

Carl Rogers was famous for developing person-centred therapy, where people could talk about their problems in a safe and supportive space. He believed everyone could grow and reach their potential through empathy and support. Rogers listened carefully, making sure people felt heard and understood.

Carl Rogers

His approach changed how therapists work and made therapy more about understanding and kindness. Rogers' methods helped many people feel better about themselves and find solutions to their problems in a non-confrontational way.

BE THE REASON SOMEONE SMILES TODAY!

Rogers' approach was like a warm hug for the heart. He showed how we can help others feel valued and understood by being kind and listening. This made it easier for people to open up and share their thoughts and feelings and then discover their own solutions. His work transformed therapy into a more caring and supportive practice.

FUN FACT

Rogers loved hiking and often found his best ideas while walking in nature. His love for the outdoors helped him stay positive and creative. He was so good at helping people understand each other and promoting peace that he was even nominated for a Nobel Peace Prize.

The doll test expert:
Mamie Phipps Clark (1917–1983)

Mamie Phipps Clark was famous for using dolls to reveal how children perceive race. She conducted the well-known "doll test", asking children to choose between dolls of different races. The children often chose White dolls over Black dolls, showing how early racism affects kids' self-esteem and how they see

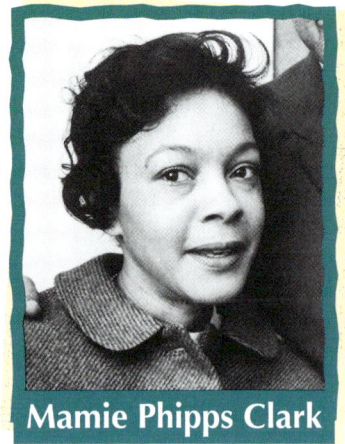

Mamie Phipps Clark

others and themselves. Clark's work was crucial in the fight against segregation in American schools. Her research helped convince the Supreme Court to end discrimination, making schools more equal for everyone.

Clark's work held up a mirror to society, showing how children learn about race and equality. Her research proved that social issues, like racism, can profoundly impact how kids feel about themselves and others, and this understanding was vital in changing unfair laws and practices. Clark's work with the doll test and her dedication to helping children showed the world that everyone deserves to feel valued and respected. Her efforts made a big difference in creating a fairer and kinder world for all kids.

FUN FACT

Clark loved helping kids so much that she and her husband founded the Northside Centre for Child Development in Harlem, US. This centre offers counselling, support and fun activities, like baking cookies, to help children feel strong and happy.

The importance of ethics in psychology

While these brilliant psychologists made incredible discoveries, they also showed how important ethics are in psychology. Ethics make sure experiments and studies are safe and respectful, and psychologists must follow ethical guidelines to protect everyone's wellbeing and rights when working with people or animals.

Take Ivan Pavlov's work with dogs and BF Skinner's experiments with animals. They showed us why treating animals kindly is crucial. Nowadays, psychologists must ensure that any experiments with animals are necessary and that the animals are well cared for.

Ethics are even more critical in human studies. Sigmund Freud's psychoanalysis involved chatting with people about their deepest thoughts and feelings.

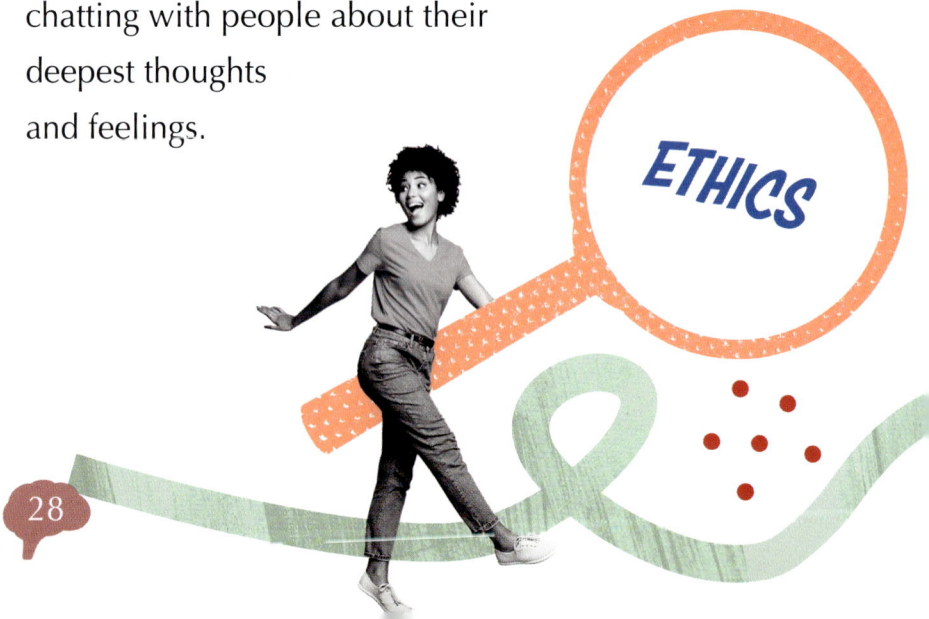

ETHICS

It's essential that psychologists keep this information private and only use it to help the person. This is called confidentiality.

Additionally, experiments must not harm participants. If a study might make someone sad or scared, psychologists must find a way to minimise this harm or choose a different method.

Ethics also ensure everyone is treated equally and fairly. Mamie Phipps Clark's work with children highlighted the need to be mindful of how social issues like racism can affect psychological wellbeing. Psychologists must constantly work to create fair and inclusive practices.

Think of ethics as a board game's rules, ensuring everyone plays fairly and no one's feelings get hurt.

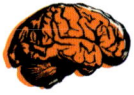

3 THE MIND AND BRAIN

What's inside your head?

Imagine having a supercomputer inside your head that controls everything you do. Guess what? You do! It's your brain, the most crucial part of your body.

The brain: your body's command centre

Your brain is the boss of your body. It tells your muscles to move, your heart to beat and your lungs to breathe. It even helps you think, learn, and feel emotions. Without your brain, nothing in your body would work.

The different parts of your brain

Your brain has different parts, each with its own job. Here are the main sections:

Cerebrum: This is the largest part of your brain. It looks like a giant walnut with lots of wrinkles. The cerebrum helps you think, remember stuff, solve problems and experience emotions. Each side of the cerebrum controls the opposite side of your body.

Cerebellum: This smaller part is at the back of your brain. It helps with balance and **coordination**. When you ride a bike or catch a ball, your cerebellum ensures you don't fall over.

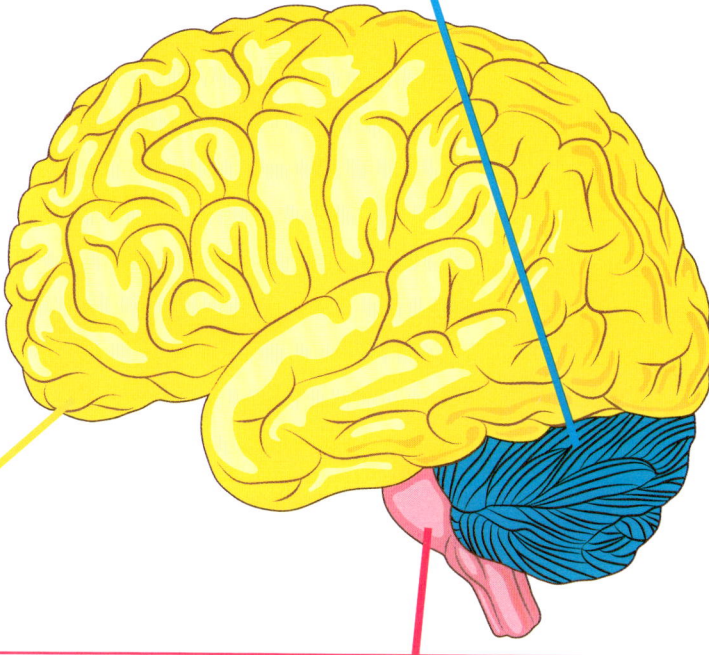

Brainstem: The brainstem is at the base of your brain and connects to your **spinal cord**. It controls your body's automatic functions, like breathing and your heartbeat.

Your brain is truly incredible, managing everything you do and think, making it the ultimate command centre.

Neurons: the brain's messengers

Your brain is made up of billions of tiny cells called neurons. Neurons send information all over your brain and body using electrical signals and special chemicals called **neurotransmitters**. Think of neurotransmitters as sprinkles of magical dust that help your brain quickly understand things and make decisions.

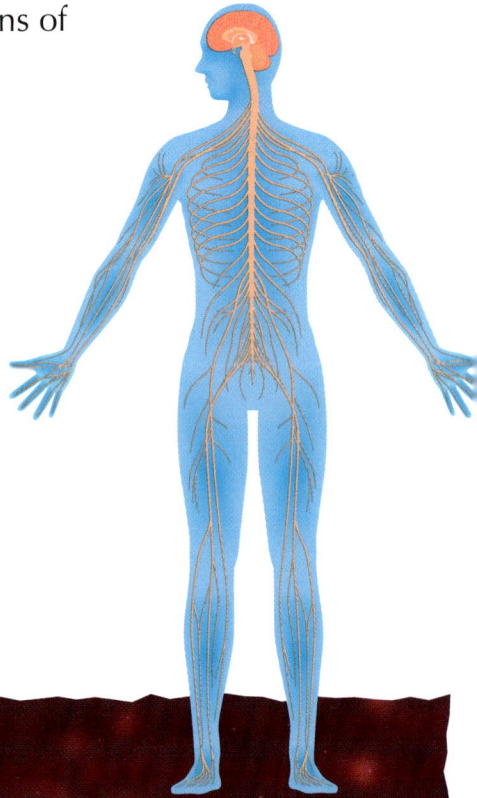

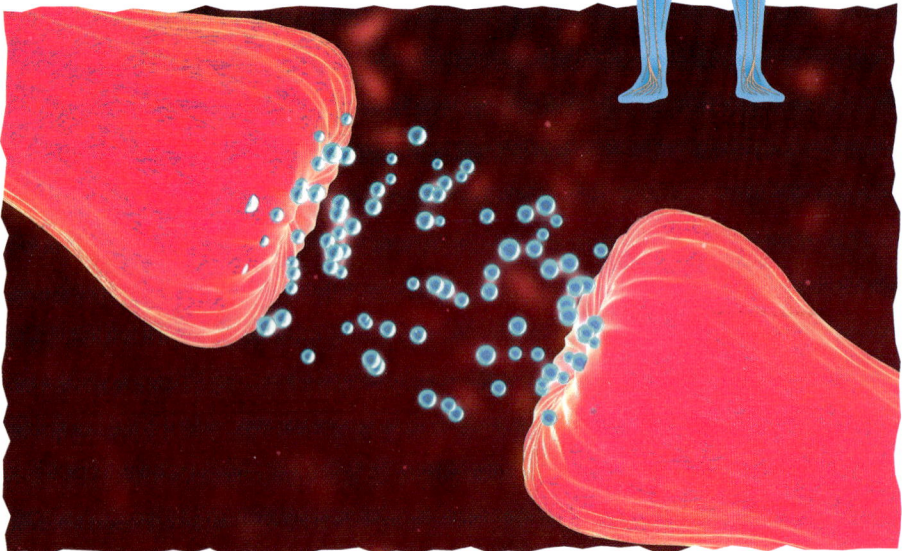

How memory works

Your brain works like a super-smart computer, storing information like the cloud does online. There are two main types of memory.

Short-term memory: This is like your brain's sticky notes. It holds information for a while, like when you remember a phone number long enough to dial it.

Long-term memory: Similar to a massive hard drive, your brain stores information for a long time. It keeps your memories of fun holidays, your best friend's birthday, and how to ride a bike.

Your brain is an expert at organising and keeping all the critical stuff you learn and experience. Different parts of your brain work together to create and manage your thoughts. For example, the amygdala helps you feel fear and excitement, while the hippocampus enables you to remember things that make you happy or sad.

Keeping your brain healthy

Taking care of your brain is super important. Here are some tips to keep it healthy.

Eat healthy foods: Foods like fruits, vegetables and fish give your brain essential nutrients. These yummy foods help your brain stay strong and intelligent.

Get plenty of sleep: Sleep helps your brain recharge and process what you've learnt during the day.

Exercise regularly: Physical activity increases blood flow to your brain, helping it stay sharp. Running, jumping and playing all help your brain to stay in shape.

Keep learning: Trying new things and solving puzzles can improve your brain. Whether reading a new book, learning a musical instrument, or figuring out a tricky puzzle, keeping your brain busy strengthens it.

Stay hydrated: Drinking water is also vital for your brain, as water keeps your brain cells happy and working well.

Relax and have fun: Taking time to relax and play helps your brain feel good. Activities like drawing, playing games and spending time with friends can make your brain experience happiness and feel refreshed.

By following these tips, you can keep your brain healthy, happy and ready for all the adventures you want to go on!

Awesome brain facts

Weighty wonder: Your brain weighs about 1.4 kilograms, as much as a small melon.

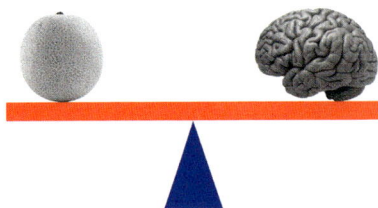

Oxygen gobbler: Even though your brain is only about 2% of your body weight, it uses around 20% of your body's oxygen and energy!

Water world: Your brain is about 75% water, so drinking water helps keep it working well.

Neural network: Your brain has about 86 billion neurons, each tiny cell sending messages to each other.

Speedy signals: Neurons in your brain can send messages up to 432 kilometres per hour – that's as fast as a bullet train!

Memory marvel: Your brain can store a huge amount of information, like a supersized library.

Dream machine: You can have up to seven dreams every night!

Lefty or righty: The left side of your brain controls the right side of your body, and the right side controls the left.

Always on: Your brain never stops working, even when asleep! It's always busy, keeping you alive and well.

Your brain helps you do everything from thinking and feeling to moving and breathing, so understanding and taking care of it is essential for keeping it healthy and strong.

4 EMOTIONS AND BEHAVIOUR: THE FEELINGS FACTORY

Understanding your emotions

Have you ever felt happy when you see your friends or angry when something doesn't go your way? These are feelings, also known as emotions. They are a big part of being human and come from your brilliant brain. Inside your brain is a special part called the limbic system, which helps create emotions.

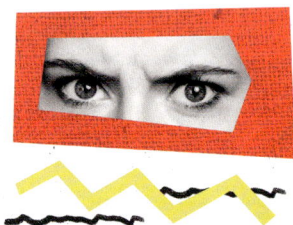

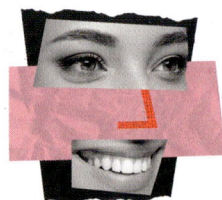

Your brain produces all kinds of emotions, such as happiness, sadness, anger, fear, surprise, disgust and excitement – it's a long list!

Scientists like BF Skinner and Carl Rogers studied these emotions and behaviours to help us understand them better. Skinner discovered that rewards and consequences can change our actions, while Rogers found that kindness and listening to people can help them feel better.

Emotions help you react to what's happening around you. For example, happiness makes you smile and want to spend time with others, while anger might make you want to fix something that's bothering you.

So, next time you feel happy, sad or angry, remember it's your brain at work, and there are always new things to learn about how you can help your extraordinary mind.

Why do we feel the way we do?

Emotions are your brain's way of responding to things happening around you. They can be influenced by your experiences, memories, and even what other people say or do. Here are some examples.

Fear: Have you ever felt terrified of spiders or heights? Fear is a normal emotion that helps protect us from danger. If you got startled by a dog when you were younger, you might still feel scared of dogs now. This shows how past experiences are remembered and can make our emotions stronger.

Happiness: Seeing your friends or playing your favourite game can make you happy because your brain releases endorphins, chemicals that make you feel good. Additionally, your brain releases dopamine, another chemical which helps you recognise and remember these activities as positive experiences, encouraging you to seek them out again.

Anger: You might feel angry when someone interrupts you during a game. This is your brain's way of telling you that something isn't right. If you're furious because you're hurt or left out, you might behave in a way that makes others think you're not being nice, without them actually knowing the real reason.

Understanding why we feel certain emotions can help us to handle them better. By learning about our feelings and talking about them, we can manage them more easily and help others understand us, too.

Understanding your behaviour

Behaviour is when you respond to something by your actions; sometimes, this reaction is because of your feelings. Recognising your behaviour can help you make better choices and react to situations well, and better understand the reasons behind your actions. For example, if you feel angry, instead of shouting at others who made you furious, you can reflect on a better response.

Here are some questions to ask yourself to understand why you behave the way you do.

What am I thinking and how am I feeling? Pay attention to your thoughts and feelings in different situations. Are you happy, sad, excited, or nervous? How are these feelings influencing your behaviour?

How are others influencing me?
Consider how other people are affecting your behaviour. Are you behaving like your friends, your family, or someone you admire?

What can I do about it? Focus on what you can control; accept what you can't.

Practise self-control: When you notice yourself behaving in a way you don't like, take a moment to pause and think before acting. Ask yourself if your behaviour is helping you or anyone else.

Seek support: If you struggle to change your behaviour, ask for help. Talk to a trusted adult, like a parent or teacher.

Most schools want everyone to be kind, respectful and responsible. They teach kids that being good to others helps you grow and improves your community. By thinking about how your actions affect others and always trying your best, you can help make your school a place where everyone feels rewarded and respected.

How social media can influence your emotions and behaviour

What is social media?

It's not just real life that can influence how you feel: social media can greatly impact your emotions and behaviour. Social media are online platforms where people share and connect with others through posts, pictures and messages. Seeing photos and posts from friends can make us cheerful, but sometimes, it can make us feel left out or miserable, especially if they're doing something that you want to be doing. Here are some ways social media can influence our emotions and behaviours.

Positive influence:

Social media can be a great way to connect with friends and family, share your achievements, learn new things and get support.

Negative influence:

Sometimes, comparing people's fantastic lives (like some "social media influencers") to our own can make us feel bad about ourselves. Remember that people often only post the nice things, not the whole picture.

Mindful use: Be aware of how social media makes you feel and act. If it makes you feel bad, take a break and do something you enjoy offline.

By understanding your emotions and noticing how social media affects your responses, you can better handle difficult situations like bullying and friendship ups and downs. Remember, asking for help and discussing your feelings with someone you trust is OK.

Why we do what we do: the cool science of social psychology

Have you ever wondered why people do what they do and why some kids hang out in groups while others prefer to be alone? Social psychology is the study of these behaviours.

Social psychology helps us understand why we act the way we do around others. For instance, it can explain why we might feel nervous speaking in front of the class or enjoy being part of a team. Social psychology helps us understand the hidden reasons behind why we think, feel and act the way we do in social situations.

The power of the group

Imagine all your friends have dyed their hair green and keep talking about how cool it is and how great it feels to be part of a special group.

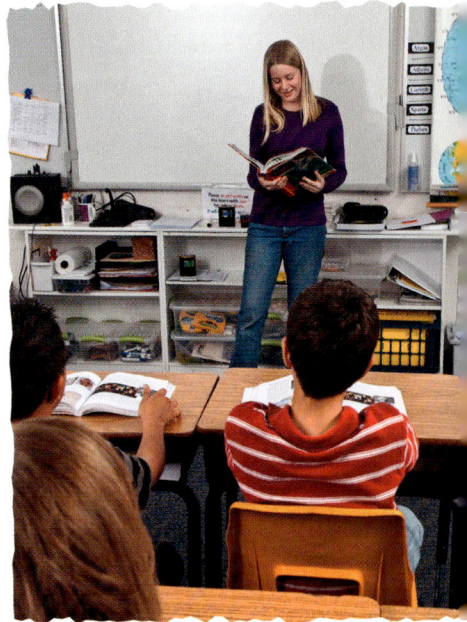

When you hang out, they always mention how good it is to have green hair and how it makes them feel connected. Even though you're unsure, you start thinking maybe you should dye your hair green too, so you don't miss out. That's peer pressure – when you feel influenced by what others are doing because you want to fit in and feel the same sense of belonging.

Social psychology helps us understand why we sometimes go along with the group, even when we want to do something different. Knowing this can help us to make better choices and understand ourselves and others.

The mirror effect

Ever notice how you act differently around family and friends? That's because of social roles. For instance, with family, you might be responsible, but with friends, you could be the class clown.

Copycats are cool

Humans love to copy each other, which is known as social learning. For instance, if you see your friend trying a new trick with a football, you might want to try it, too. We learn by watching others.

Be yourself

Being who you are is something that only you can do! When you're kind, empathetic and generous, you shine brightly. For example, standing up for a friend or helping someone in need shows your inner hero. Studies in social psychology show that doing good deeds and thinking positively when possible can make you happier and inspire even more kindness.

Remember, your unique self and positive actions are your true superpowers.

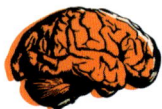

5 SELF-PSYCHOLOGY

Take care of your thoughts, feelings and actions

Remember Mary Whiton Calkins, the woman who founded self-psychology? She taught us that taking care of yourself is super important. Self-psychology is all about understanding your own thoughts, feelings and actions. It means doing things that make you happy, healthy and strong.

Self-care can be simple, like eating nutritious foods, drinking lots of water, and getting plenty of sleep. It also means exercising regularly and taking breaks to relax. When you care for your body, your mind feels better, too!

SELF-CARE

Being kind to yourself is like being your own best friend. Sometimes, we might make mistakes or feel down, but it's important to remember that we can learn from them. Instead of being hard on yourself, think about everything you do well. Hug yourself and say, "I am awesome just the way I am!"

Positive thoughts can make a huge difference in how you feel and act. When you think positively, you can do impressive things. So, always take time for yourself and enjoy being uniquely you!

Taking care of your mind and body

Creativity

Being creative is a fun way to take care of your mind. Drawing, painting, writing stories or playing a musical instrument are great ways to express yourself – it doesn't matter if you're very good or not! You can explore your imagination and have lots of fun doing creative activities.

Compassion

Compassion means being kind to yourself and others. When you understand why you feel a certain way, you can figure out how to feel better. For example, you can practise deep breathing to calm down if you feel nervous about a test. Knowing yourself helps you make good choices and be content.

Courage

Remember, you are enough just the way you are. You don't need to be perfect to be unique. Everyone has their own special talents and qualities that make them exceptional. Celebrate who you are and be proud of yourself whenever you do something kind, respectful and polite. When you believe in yourself, you can achieve many more things and earn more rewards for your collection. Always be proud of your achievements, big or small.

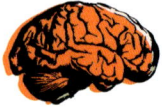

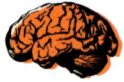

6 FUN MIND TRICKS

Optical illusions

Have you ever looked at something with a friend, and seen something completely different to them? It might have been an optical illusion. These mind-blowing visual puzzles trick your eyes and brain, making you see things in completely different ways.

Why optical illusions are important

Optical illusions are not just fun and games – they also teach us a lot about how our brains work. Scientists use illusions to study **perception**, learning how our brains process visual information and make sense of the world. This research can help us understand vision problems and develop new technologies.

In the following few pages, you'll find a selection of the most astonishing illusions that will leave you questioning everything you see.

Duck-Rabbit Illusion

One of the most famous optical illusions is the Duck-Rabbit Illusion.

This playful image, published by psychologist Joseph Jastrow in the late 19th century, shows either a duck facing left or a rabbit facing right. Depending on how you look at it, your brain can switch between seeing the duck or the rabbit. Show the image to your friends and find out who sees the duck first and who sees the rabbit.

Young Woman or Old Woman Illusion

The Young Woman or Old Woman Illusion was first published by cartoonist William Ely Hill in 1915.

The picture can be seen as either an older woman with her head down or a young woman facing away. Most people can't see both versions at the same time. Can you switch between seeing both? Which one do you see first?

The Impossible Trident

Check out the Impossible Trident! This puzzling illusion looks like a three-pronged fork, but when you follow the prongs, they seem to split and merge in impossible ways. It's a shape that can't actually exist in real life, and it's a great example of how our brains try to make sense of 2-D drawings as 3-D objects.

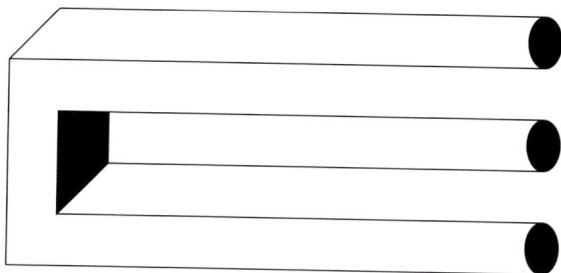

Draw your own

Try drawing an impossible shape like the trident or another illusion such as the Penrose Triangle.

Get creative and see how many impossible shapes you can come up with, while learning about how different brains work.

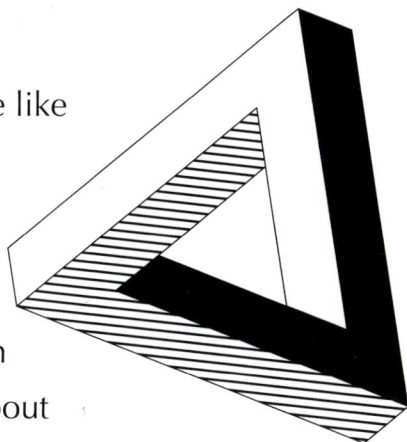

The Ames Room

Have you ever wanted to grow high up into the air or shrink down into the ground? The Ames Room illusion makes this possible! It's a specially constructed room where one corner is much closer to the viewer than the other. When people stand in different parts of the room, they appear to be wildly different sizes, even though they're the same size. This shows how the way we look at things and the details around them can trick our brains into seeing things that aren't really there.

Create an illusion

Equipment: camera

1. Choose a space: Find a room or an area with enough space for someone to stand at the back and the front.

2. Position the people: Have one person stand close to the camera at the front and another person stand far away at the back.

3. Set up the camera: Place the camera at a fixed point near the front and ensure it's at eye level with the person at the front.

4. Capture the illusion: Look through the lens or take a photo. The person at the back will appear much smaller, creating the illusion of different sizes.

The Café Wall Illusion

The Café Wall Illusion is a mind-boggler. It looks like the lines between the bricks are sloping, but they're actually perfectly straight and parallel. This illusion tricks our perception of angles and contrasts.

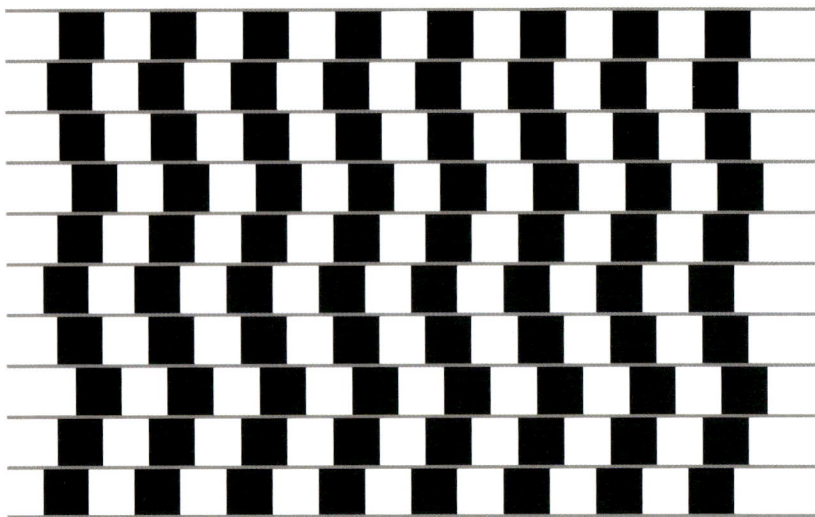

The Müller-Lyer Illusion

In the Müller-Lyer Illusion, two lines of the same length appear different because of the arrows at the ends. One line has arrows pointing inwards, making it look shorter, while the other has arrows pointing outwards, making it look longer, showing how additional details can completely change how we see identical things.

Measure to believe: Grab yourself a ruler and carefully measure the lines. You'll be amazed that they're actually the same length!

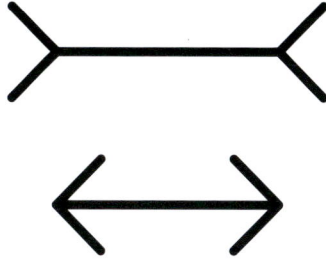

The Checker Shadow Illusion

The Checker Shadow Illusion, created by Edward Adelson, tricks your brain with shadows. In this illusion, a checkerboard has dark and light squares, and a shadow falls over part of it. Even though two squares (A and B) look like different shades, they are the same colour.

Why do optical illusions trick us?

Did you enjoy the optical illusions? So, why do these optical illusions captivate us? It's all because of how our brains work. Our brains are like computers, constantly processing visual information and trying to understand what we see. When we look at optical illusions, our brains get confused by the tricky images and struggle to decide what we're actually seeing.

The brain's shortcut system

Our brains love shortcuts. They quickly try to recognise patterns and familiar shapes to save time and energy. However, optical illusions disrupt these shortcuts, presenting images our brains can't easily categorise. This confusion makes optical illusions so intriguing and fun to look at.

The power of context

Optical illusions also show us the power of perspective. The surrounding details in an image can change how we see the main image. For example, in the Checker Shadow Illusion, a shadow cast over a checkerboard makes two squares of the same colour appear different. The shadow and surrounding squares trick our brains into seeing different shades.

The next time you spot an optical illusion, share it with your friends and see if they get tricked, too!

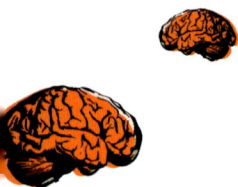

7 WHAT MAKES US TERRIFIED?

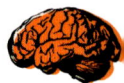

Understanding phobias

Have you ever felt scared of something, even though you knew it couldn't hurt you? Maybe it was a tiny spider, a high place, or a loud thunderstorm. This kind of intense fear is called a phobia, a big fear of something that might not be as dangerous as you think it is.

What is a phobia?

A phobia is a strong and unreasonable fear of an object or situation that poses little or no actual danger but causes anxiety and avoidance. There are many different types of phobias. For example, someone with a phobia of dogs might feel very scared when seeing one, even if it's just a picture of a small, friendly-looking dog.

Some well-known phobias include: claustrophobia, the fear of small, enclosed spaces; arachnophobia, the fear of spiders; and coulrophobia, the fear of clowns. Even though these fears might seem irrational to others, they can be very real and distressing for the person experiencing them.

Why do we develop phobias?

Phobias often start in childhood, but they can develop at any age. There are a few reasons why someone might develop a phobia.

Bad experiences: Sometimes, a phobia starts because of a scary or bad experience. For example, if you fell from a stepladder when you were little, you might develop a fear of heights.

Learnt behaviour: Watching someone else be terrified of something can also make you scared of it. For example, if a parent or carer is terrified of heights, a child might also learn to fear heights.

How the brain creates phobias

When we have a scary experience, our brain helps create phobias. The amygdala, a part of the brain, makes strong emotional memories. This means that when something similar happens again, we might feel scared, even if it's not really dangerous. The brain is trying to protect us by remembering things that frightened us before. However, sometimes it overreacts, making us afraid of things that aren't actually harmful. This is how a phobia is created.

There are many types of phobias, but they usually fall into two main categories. **Specific phobias** are fears of objects or situations, like snakes, heights, or flying.

Social phobia is a fear of social situations where you might feel embarrassed or judged (criticised or watched), such as speaking in front of the class or meeting new people.

How do phobias affect us?

Phobias can be sticky and tricky. They might make you feel very anxious when you encounter the thing you're afraid of. You might try very hard to avoid it, making it difficult to do everyday things. But is there a way to manage them?

The good news is that there are ways to cope with and even overcome phobias.

Talk about it: Telling a trusted adult or friend about your fear can help a lot. They can support you and might have ideas to make you feel better.

Learn about your fear: Sometimes, learning more about what scares you can make it less scary. For example, understanding that a tiny spider can't hurt you can help reduce your fear.

Gradual exposure: This means slowly getting used to what scares you, a little bit at a time. For example, if you're afraid of cats, you could start by looking at pictures, then watching videos of cats, and eventually being near a small, friendly cat.

Relaxation techniques: Take deep breaths, picture a peaceful beach, or try some fun relaxation tricks to help your mind and body feel calm when you're confronted with the thing you're afraid of.

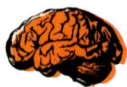

8 JOBS IN PSYCHOLOGY

Have you ever wondered who helps people when they feel sad, worried or confused? There are loads of people who have trained for years and do just that! Each job helps us understand the mind and makes the world a better place. Whether you love solving mysteries, helping others, or exploring how our brains work, psychology careers cover many people, experiences and skills. Let's check out what they do.

Psychologist

A psychologist is like a private detective for feelings and thoughts. They study how our minds work and why we feel the way we do. Psychologists help people understand their emotions and find ways to feel better. They might work in schools or hospitals or have their own clinical practice. Psychologists usually have a doctorate in Psychology and need to be licensed to be a psychologist. That means they've completed all of the studies needed and can officially work in that role.

Therapist

A therapist is like a friendly helper who talks with people to help them feel better when feeling down, worried or stressed. They're really good listeners who are able to offer a supportive environment for you to be honest, where you know you won't be judged. Therapists help children and grown-ups with all kinds of problems by teaching them new ways to think about and deal with their problems. Therapists often have special training, such as a Master's degree in Counselling, Social Work or Psychology.

Psychotherapist

A psychotherapist uses special talking techniques to help people understand their feelings and solve their problems. Psychotherapists often have advanced training to address more complex emotional and psychological issues. They usually need a Master's degree or higher in Psychology, Counselling, Social Work, or a related field, and must be accredited (similar to licensed) to act as a psychotherapist.

Psychiatrist

A psychiatrist is like a brain doctor! They know all about how the brain works and can even prescribe medicine to help people feel better. Psychiatrists can chat with people about their feelings, just like therapists, but they can also check if something in the brain needs special treatment. They need to go to medical school to become doctors and then get special training in Psychiatry. They also need to be certified (similar to licensed or accredited).

Counsellor

You can talk to a counsellor when you need help figuring out your feelings or making decisions.

Counsellors are like guides who work in schools to help students with their problems or in offices to help people with family or work issues. They give great advice and support to help people find their way. Counsellors usually need a Diploma in Counselling or a related subject, and must be certified or registered as a counsellor.

There are many experts in the field of psychology. Psychotherapists and psychologists are like feelings detectives, studying a lot and practising with experts. Psychiatrists are like brain superheroes, attending medical school and getting extra training. Counsellors and therapists are friendly guides who earn special degrees and learn by helping others. To succeed in psychology, you need a big heart and a desire to help people.

Mental health first aider

Introducing a cool new job title: a mental health first aider! These helpers are trained to assist someone when they're having an emotional health crisis, like feeling super panicked or scared. They give first aid to the mind, just like regular first aiders do for the body. They support and help you feel better until you can see a professional, like a counsellor, psychologist or psychiatrist.

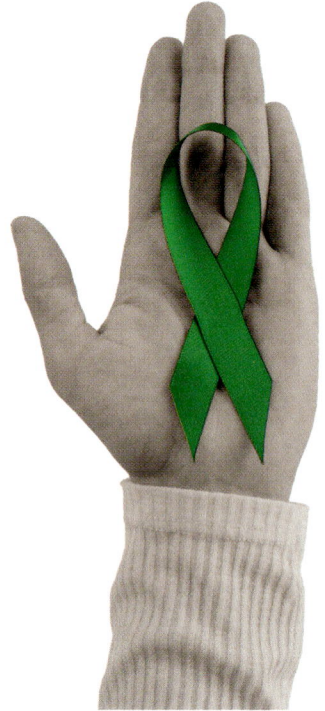

Neuropsychologist

Neuropsychologists are brain explorers! They study how our brains work, and help people with brain injuries or conditions like memory loss. Imagine them as detectives solving the brain's mysteries and ensuring everything works just right. They need a doctorate degree in Psychology or Neuropsychology, and they usually complete specialised training in brain science. They also need to be certified to practise.

All these wonderful people are like a team of heroes, each with their own unique superpowers to help us feel our best. They listen to us, understand our feelings, and provide solutions for happiness and wellbeing. Whether it's talking about our day, solving a big problem, or getting help from a doctor, these people have dedicated their lives to supporting us.

With these incredible careers in psychology, you can find a job that excites you and makes a difference in the world. One day, you might become one of these heroes, helping others and exploring the fascinating world of the mind.

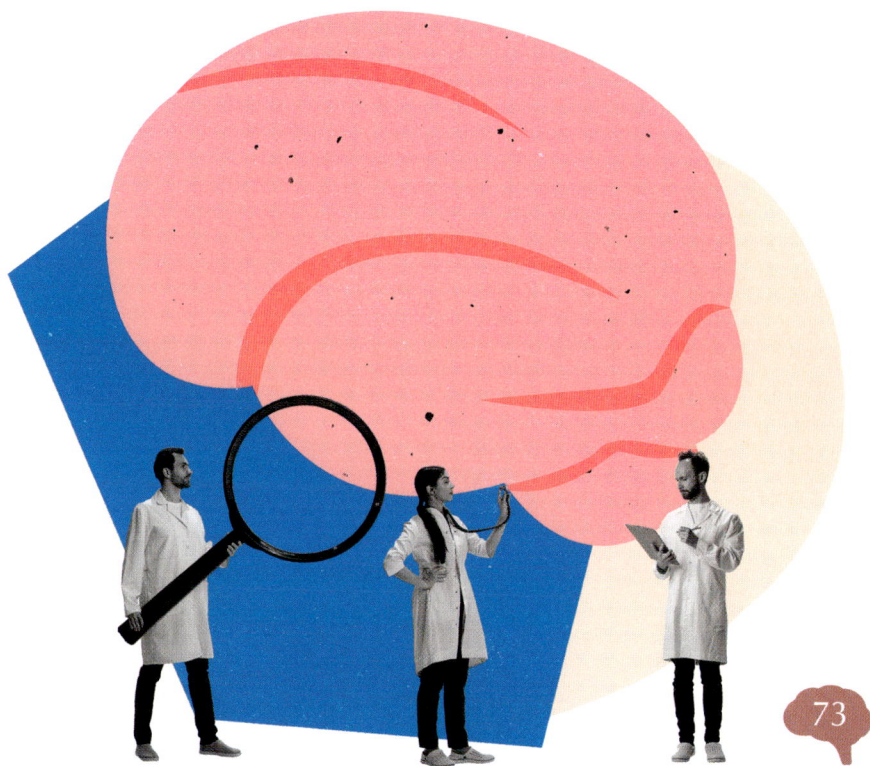

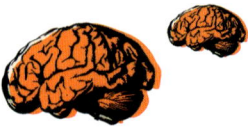

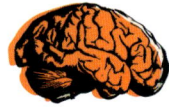

9 CONCLUSION

Is your brain exhausted from learning all about itself? We learnt how our brains work like supercomputers, controlling everything we do, from thinking and feeling to moving and breathing. We met brilliant mind detectives like Ivan Pavlov, Sigmund Freud, Anna Freud, Melanie Klein, and more, who uncovered the secrets of the human mind.

We explored how our emotions and behaviours shape who we are and how optical illusions trick our brains into seeing things that aren't there. That's the fun part! We also learnt about different types of phobias and how to manage them. You've picked up key tips for your emotional and mental wellbeing.

Remember, your brain is like a super warrior, filled with incredible powers. By understanding how our minds work, we can live happier, healthier lives. Stay curious, keep learning, and never stop exploring the fascinating world of psychology. Your mind is astonishing and, remember, so are you!

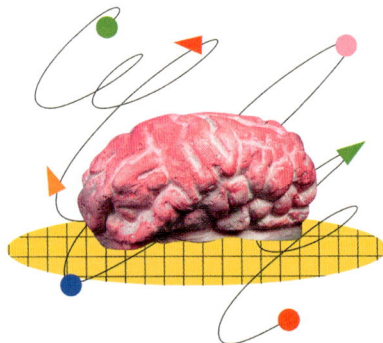

GLOSSARY

archaeology the study of humans and the past by looking at objects that are found from the time

conditioning learning to connect one thing with another, like Pavlov's dogs drooling when they heard a bell

conscious self the part of ourselves, including our actions and thoughts, that we're aware of

coordination how well you can use different parts of your body at the same time

emotions feelings like happiness, sadness, anger and fear that come from your brain

empathy understanding and sharing someone else's feelings

exclusion someone or something being left out of something on purpose

insight a deep understanding of something

laboratory a place for conducting scientific experiments, and studying scientific theories

neurotransmitters special chemicals in your brain that help send messages between neurons

perception how your brain understands what you see, hear and feel

pioneer someone who is the first person to explore or
    do something

psychoanalysis a way to understand your deepest
    thoughts and feelings by discussing your dreams and
    past experiences

spinal cord a long tube connecting your brain and lower
    back, carrying messages from your brain to your body

unconscious something that happens without you knowing
    about it

INDEX

TIPS FOR DAILY WELLBEING

Eat healthy foods
Include many fruits, vegetables, and whole grains.

Exercise regularly
Aim for at least 30 minutes of daily physical activity.

Get enough sleep
Get 8–10 hours of sleep each night.

Practise mindfulness
Take a few minutes daily to meditate or do deep breathing exercises.

Stay hydrated

Drink plenty of water throughout the day.

Creative activities

Try drawing, painting, writing stories, or playing a musical instrument to express yourself and have fun.

Find activities

Engage in fun activities like volunteering and helping those in need.

Connect with others

Spend time with friends and family to feel supported and happy.

Take breaks

Regular breaks from devices and schoolwork help us relax and recharge.

🐾 Ideas for reading 🐾

Gill Matthews
Primary Literacy Consultant

Reading objectives:
- check that the book makes sense to them, discussing their understanding and exploring the meaning of words in context
- summarise the main ideas drawn from more than one paragraph, identifying key details that support the main ideas
- retrieve, record and present information from non-fiction

Spoken language objectives:
- ask relevant questions to extend their understanding and knowledge
- participate in discussions, presentations, performances, role play, improvisations and debates

Curriculum links: Relationships Education: caring friendships; respectful relationships

Interest words: extraordinary, fascinating, ultimate, incredible

Build a context for reading
- Ask children to read the title on the front cover. Explore their knowledge and understanding of psychology.
- Ask why they think the book has specific doodles on the cover.
- Read the back-cover blurb. Ask children what they think they are going to find out from the book.
- Point out that this is an information book. Ask what features the children expect to find in the book and what reading strategies they might use.
- Ask children to turn to the contents page and to identify the chapter they think will give an overview of the book.

Understand and apply reading strategies
- Read pp2–3 aloud then demonstrate how to briefly summarise the information on these pages. Explain that summarising a piece of text can help to understand it.
- Give children the opportunity to read and summarise pp4–5.